2020 Keep America Great, the Artistic Case for Trump

By Matthew Breer

ISBN: 1725911477
ISBN-13: 978-1725911475

DEDICATION

The purpose of this book is to provide a perspective artistically and opinionated. Also to directly address why in believing we should all vote trump 2020. As an artist, it's important to me to associate this volume of artwork with the patriotism that Trump has helped to bring back to the people of the United States. Dedicated the people of the United States of America, our men and women of the military, and to the president himself for bringing hope where there was none.

ACKNOWLEDGMENTS

Special Thanks to Donald Trump, Alexis De Tocqueville, Hon. John T. Morgan, Hon. John J. Ingalls whose work made this publication possible.

Q

We the People

In all the reasons for electing trump the one that stands out most clearly is his support of the constitution and respect for law and order. In that this artwork we the people clearly illustrates my belief in supporting trump for the sole purpose of defending our Constitution. In the eleven years that separated the signing of the Declaration of the Independence to the ordination of our written Constitution, the great minds of America were focused on the study of the principles of government that were essential to the preservation of the liberties which had been won at such a great cost, with heroic labors and sacrifices. Their studies were conducted in view of the imperfections that experience had developed in the governments of the world, and they were, therefore, practical and thorough in creating this document.

When the Constitution was perfected and established, a new form of government was created, but it was neither speculative nor experimental as to the principles on which it was based. If they were true principles, as they were, the government founded upon them was destined to a life and an influence that would continue while the liberties it was intended to preserve should be valued by everyone both young and old. Those liberties had been earned from reluctant monarchs in many contests, in many countries, were grouped into creeds and established in ordinances sealed with blood, in many great struggles of the people from around the world. In other words, they were not new to the people but duly earned throw sweet and blood. They were true theories, but no government had been previously established for the great purpose of their preservation and enforcement. So it becomes imperative that we the people support trump so as to preserve the Constitution.

Freedom

Freedom is like a stamp once achieved it helps to convey the message where ever the message goes over time the constitution of the U.S.A. has come under fire from the left and its fundamental purpose questioned by the left, staining the great U.S.A., And that attack continues today. But because of Donald Trump and his choices in Supreme Court justices, we can rest assured that the constitution and the United States of America will remain strong because Trump has chosen and will continue to choose defenders our constitution and our constitutional rights ensuring freedom for all those who stand for the U.S.A. So for this is another reason I hope we re-elect trump in 2020 and keep America great.

Independence Hall

Independence Hall where the constitution was created stands as a testimony to the patriotic spirit of America. Many a speech and protest has occurred on the grounds of independence hall both for trump and against, but it's important to remember what this represents, which is the very foundation on which our nation rests the constitution, in that freedom rings, throw the voices of the people and it becomes imperative that we as citizens must take action to re-elect trump, so vote trump 2020.

Pride

The pride in our flag and comfort that the American people enjoy is the consciousness of victory over a false narrative that the left and mainstream media has used to oppress the right, this victory gives joy to the true American, whose patriotism combined with the essence of the American dream under the leadership of the 47th president of the United States, will only serve to help re-elect Donald Trump to another term, and bring more prosperity to the American people. So throw pride in our flag, our country it will be in support of the red white and blue that we will Keep America great!

Renewed Pride

Trump has renewed the pride of the United States throw the power of the people. That is to say, trump has instilled new life and pride for America, over the course of time Americas influence and prestige has been slipping. However, under the direction of Donald Trump, the United States of America is showing a renewed sense of pride and is in good hands.

47th president of the United States
Donald Trump

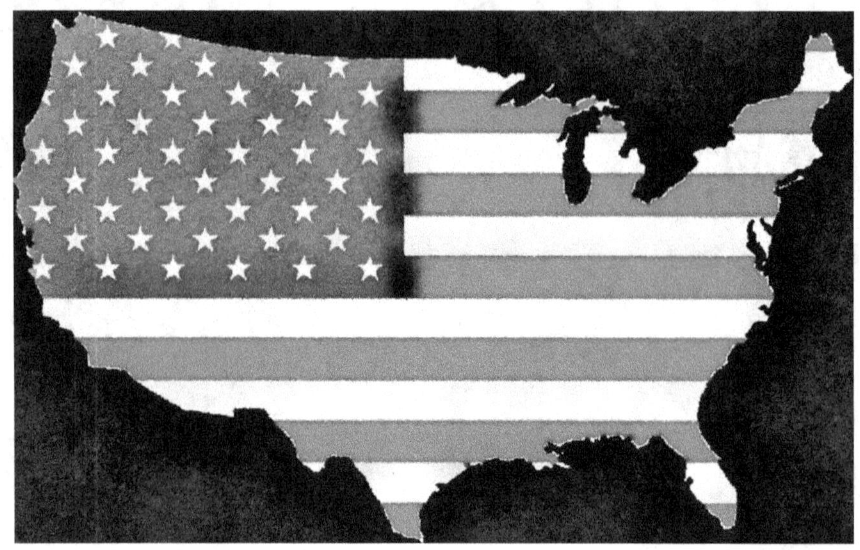

United under one flag

The left yet will surely do their part to vilify whoever stands in their path. There are many who have a strong conviction that no government can resist these internal leftist forces, when, they are directed to its destruction by bad men or unreasoning mobs, but there is hope and it came in the form of the billionaire businessman who gave up his lifestyle to "Make America great again". Our government is unequal in its ability to accomplish anything throw the labors of its people. However, the left will continue to assault the right even though the assault is thoroughly desperate. Those on the right can additionally find solace that peace, order, and prosperity, in the face of any difficulties, can be found in the Constitution and the principles on which it was founded. So we must re-elect Donald trump.

Vote America

Back before president Trump took office many on the left took offence and even tried to slander the presidents slogan "Make America Great again" suggesting America was never great, or even perverting it in to a race thing, as the left put it "make America white again" when the truth is Donald Trump the most pro-black president in history, if you asked him he would probably say Abraham Lincoln was the most pro-black president. For a long time African American citizens have been strictly a Democratic Party majority, however, under trump, this has gone throw a shift. With movements such as #walkaway where massive amounts of people are leaving the Democratic Party trumps re-election looks better and better. Many of the people walking away from the Democratic Party are from every walk of life, but with all-time record low unemployment for all American communities who can blame them, after all, if history has proven anything those who have jobs tend to be happier than those who don't. So go out and do your part and vote.

It is evident to all alike that a great Republican revolution is going on amongst us, but there are two opinions as to its nature and consequences. To some, it appears to be a horrendous thing to have Trump as our president, and to others, like myself it is the most logical most patriotic course of action. That is the majority of the left see the trump presidency as the end of the world or that is how the media portrays the left. So when the left honestly believes it's the end of the world. But the problem arises when the sun comes up and it wasn't the end of the world and trump is doing a great job and their whole worldview is destroyed. So the left continues to go after frame lie literally anything to make him look bad, however after all is said and done nothing really sticks to trump.

Revolution

In many communities, there are those who love Trump and those who hate him. It is my discernment that it is the lefts intention to turn brother against brother. The left has even gone as far to insight revolution with groups like Antifa and Black Lives Matter and many other leftist groups whose actions are more like terrorist groups than groups that are for the good of the nation. Zealous people may be found amongst us whose minds are turned against Trump possibly because he is not perfect, but to these people, I would like to say do not judge a man by his past but by his actions.

There is no country in the world where the great revolution or movement which I am speaking of seems to not have had an effect. It is not, then, merely to satisfy a legitimate curiosity that I have created this volume of patriotic artwork, but in support of the fundamental principles of our country and the constitution, which emboldened me to support Trump for re-election in 2020.

Principles

War and Cambodia

There seems to be a large number of people who are against trump, and it appears against America its self, some even wishing harm on our nation, even wishing for our economy to fail, or a war to break out just to justify their opinions that the world is going to end. When in reality it's their parties own policies that would bring the end of the world much closer to reality. Very few

Democrats seen to know the recent past (late 1970's) in regards to socialism, for instance pol pot and Cambodia, where the socialist (communist) regime killed millions in the name of progress killing people just because they had to wear glasses or educators among other things, and for the most part it all started with the confiscation of guns a second amendment right that the left has been trying for decades do away with. Being highly educated a master's in education and a year towards my doctorates and wearing glasses I would have been one of the first to go.

American pride

American values

So it is my belief in the American values that led me to support trump and the Republican Party. Trump is the future of the Democratic Republic, and with almost certainly will encounter many difficult and dangerous situations, but the principles established in the Constitution and the check upon hasty or inconsiderate legislation, and upon executive action, and the supreme courts, will be found sufficient for the safety of personal rights, hopefully, Each succeeding generation of Americans will find a new source of pride in our institutions of government, and sound reasons for patriotic effort to preserve them and to instill their teachings. After all, if Trump has done one thing he has made politics and the office of the president the talk of the town and perhaps inspired generations of Americans to go into politics.

It is my sincerest hope that the artwork and words here have inspired you to go out and vote for trump and keep America great!

But now that you've made it to the end have you discovered the hidden clues in plain sight.
Remember where we go one, we go all!
Don't let our inability to learn or remember the past be our downfall.